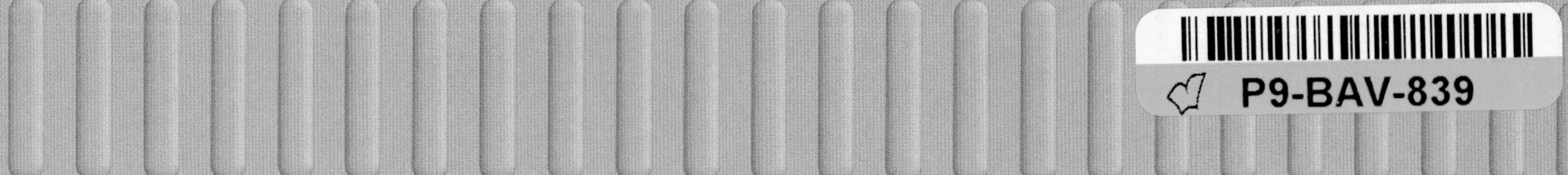

NEW TECHNOLOGY

food technology

Ian Graham

Smart Apple Media

This book has been published in cooperation with Evans Publishing Group.

Published in the United States by
Smart Apple Media, an imprint of
Black Rabbit Books
P.O. Box 3263, Mankato, Minnesota 56002

Printed in China

Library of Congress Cataloging-in-Publication Data

Graham, Ian, 1953–
Food technology / Ian Graham.
p. cm.—(Smart Apple Media. New technology)
Includes index.
Summary: "Describes new technologies used in food production such as gene technology, farming technology and robots, nanotech, packaging, and discusses the implications of using these technologies"—Provided by publisher.
ISBN 978-1-59920-162-7
1. Food industry and trade—Juvenile literature. 2. Agricultural innovations—Juvenile literature. I. Title.
TP370.3.G73 2009
664—dc22

2008000438

Credits
Series Editor: Paul Humphrey
Editor: Gianna Williams
Designer: Keith Williams
Production: Jenny Mulvanny
Picture researchers: Rachel Tisdale and Laura Embriaco
Consultant: Chris W. Edwards, Head of Food and Dairy Technology, Reaseheath College

Acknowledgements
Title page: Scott Olson/Getty Images; p.6 Malcolm Romain/istockphoto.com; p.7 Robert Wallis/Corbis; p.9 Marco Volpi/istockphoto.com; p.10 David Gray/Reuters/Corbis; p.11 Scott Olson/Getty Images; p.12 Eddie Cheng/EPA/Corbis; p.13 Shaun Best/Reuters/Corbis; p.14 Ralph Orlowski/Reuters/Corbis; p.15 Keith Weller/USDA; pp.16 and 17 University of Warwick; p.18 Floris Leeuwenberg/ The Cover Story/Corbis; p.19 Yoshisada Nagasaka (National Agricultural Research Center, Tsukuba, Japan) and Prof. Tony Grift (University of Illinois, Dept. of Agricultural and Biological Engineering, USA); p.20 Adeline Yeo/istockphoto.com; p.21 Chris Jacobs/Columbia University; p.22 Natalie Fobes/ Corbis; p.23 Sieto Verver/ istockphoto.com; p.24 Najlah Feanny/ Corbis SABA; p.25 Brian Prechtel/USDA; p.26 Natalya Gerasimova/istockphoto.com; p.27 Andrey Pustovoy/istockphoto.com; p.28 Howard Sochurek/ Corbis; p.30 Purdue University/LIBNA; p.31 US AIR FORCE/ Science Photo Library; p.32 Altrendo/Getty Images; p.33 Gaurier/photocuisine/Corbis; p.34 Chuck Savage/Corbis; p.35 Ed Wheeler/Corbis; p.36 John Nordell/ The Christian Science Monitor/Getty Images; p.37 Hotcan® Self-heating Meals; p.38 Roderick Chen/First Light/Getty Images; p.39 PASCAL GOETGHELUCK/ Science Photo Library; p.40 Richard Hobson/istockphoto.com; p.41 PETER MENZEL/Science Photo Library; p.42 Tony Arruza/Corbis; p.43 Klaas Lingbeek van Kranen/istockphoto.com

contents

	introduction	6
CHAPTER 1	**gene** technology	8
CHAPTER 2	**down** on the farm	16
CHAPTER 3	**functional** foods	24
CHAPTER 4	**nanotech**	30
CHAPTER 5	**packaging** and preserving	34
CHAPTER 6	**science** in the kitchen	40
	conclusion	42
	glossary	44
	more information	45
	index	46

introduction

Food technology is the use of science to improve the growing, harvesting, processing, packaging, distribution, cooking, and storage of food. It makes use of the latest discoveries in science and the latest developments in technology.

The need for food The demand for food is rising rapidly, because the world's population is growing faster than ever. From the year 1500, it took about 300 years for the world's population to double to one billion. From 1800, it doubled again in only 130 years. By about 1975, only 45 years later, it had doubled again to 4 billion. There are now more than 6.6 billion people on Earth. The population is rising fastest in the developing world, where farming tends to be less productive and food technology is the most basic. Improvements in science and technology that could increase food production are most urgently needed in these places.

Modern farming is an industry that relies on high technology and big machines like this combine harvester.

This laboratory is producing seeds specially modified to suit growing conditions in India.

Food tech today The way our food is produced has changed a lot over the past few decades. Advances in genetics enable scientists to change plants and animals in order to improve the food made from them or reduce its cost. Advances in farming make it possible for fewer people to produce bigger crops from the same ground. New types of packaging keep food fresher for longer.

Do you trust food technology?
Scientists can do amazing things with food. They can use nanotechnology to change it molecule by molecule to alter its flavor, texture, or nutrition. They can treat it with radiation to kill germs or insects that would spoil it or cause disease. But all the clever science and technology counts for nothing if people will not buy the food. All new foods are thoroughly tested before they go on sale, but even so there is public concern about some of the ways in which science and technology are used to change food.

This book reveals the latest technology used in food production today and looks at the new food technology that is coming in the next few years.

CHAPTER 1
gene technology

The cells of living plants and animals contain a set of instructions, the genetic code, that controls the growth and development of the plant or animal. Scientists are learning how to change the genetic code to make better plants and animals for the food industry.

Breeding Farmers have been using genetics to change plants and animals for thousands of years without knowing it. They improved their plants and animals by breeding only from the biggest and best of them. This is called selective breeding. They also bred from different, but closely related, plants and animals. This is called cross-breeding or hybridization. Farmers and growers have used crossbreeding for about 500 years.

DNA The genetic code inside living cells is made of DNA (deoxyribonucleic acid). The long, chain-like molecules of DNA are divided into chromosomes and the chromosomes are divided into units called genes. Genes control the production of proteins, and proteins build a plant or animal and carry out its functions. In the 1970s, scientists

Rod-like chromosomes made of DNA carry the genes that control an organism's growth and development.

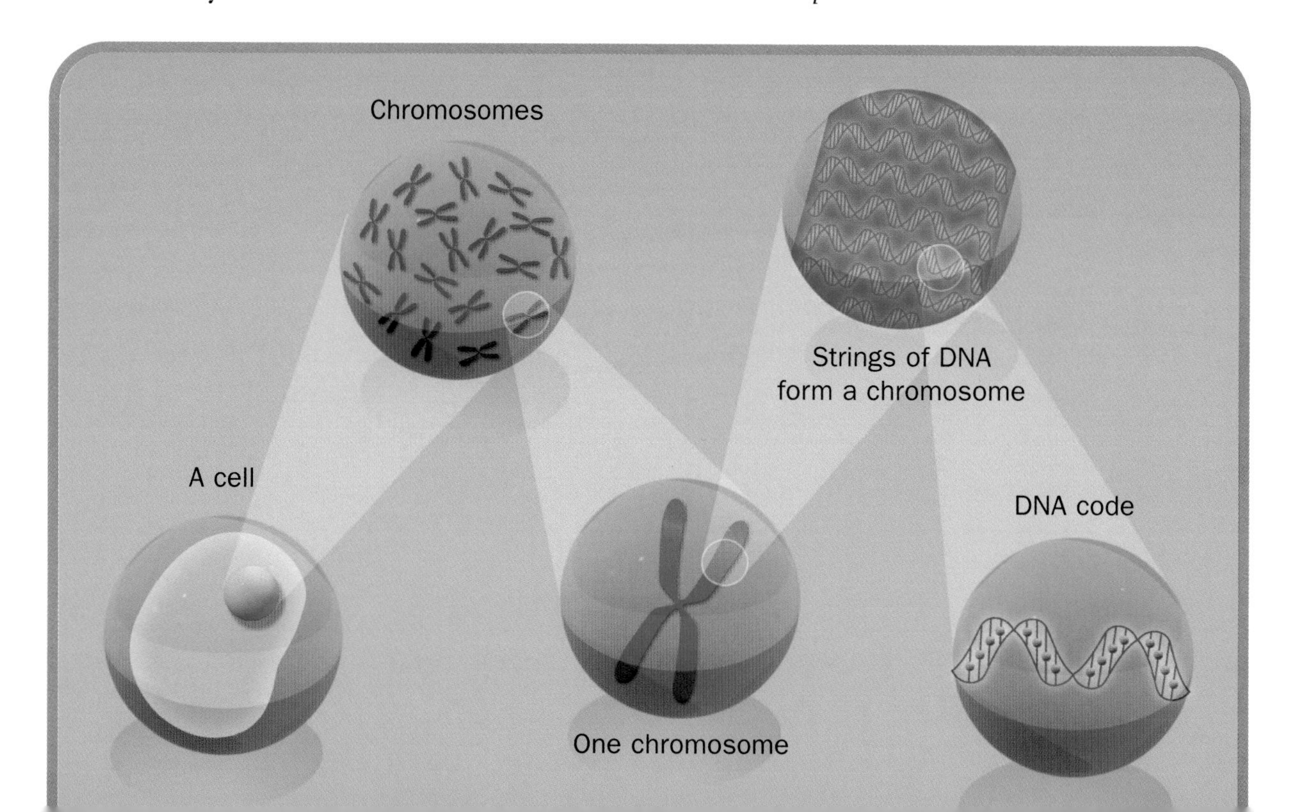

discovered that all living organisms store genetic information in the same way. This meant that it should be possible to move genes from one plant or animal to another, and even from one species to another.

HOW IT WORKS

When scientists find a useful feature in a plant, they look for the gene that produces it. They cut the gene out of the plant's DNA and insert it into bacteria. Bacteria are used because they multiply quickly, making lots of copies of the new gene, and they are also very good at getting inside living cells. Common soil bacteria called *agrobacteria tumefaciens* are often used. Viruses are used, too. The bacteria or viruses are allowed to infect the plant, or they may be injected straight into the plant cells by shooting them in with a special gun. Pieces of the plant containing cells with the new genes are then cut out and grown into new plants with the new genes. Transferring genes into animal cells is done by injecting the new genetic material directly into the nuclei of individual cells with a very fine needle.

GM crops Selective breeding and hybridization take a long time and they often fail to produce the desired results. A farmer or grower can't be certain which genes will be passed on to the next generation. A new plant bred to have bigger fruit, for example, might also catch a disease more easily or rot faster. Scientists try to get rid of this uncertainty by transferring only the genes for the features they want. Plants and animals whose genes have been changed are known as genetically modified organisms (GMOs), and crops whose genes have been changed are also known as GM crops. The first GM

These potatoes come from a genetically modified crop.

WHAT'S NEXT?

Plants need water to survive and grow. By modifying plants genetically, it is possible to produce plants that need less water. This may enable crops to be grown in ground that would normally be too dry for them. In the early 2000s, Australia suffered the worst drought on record. Rivers dried to a trickle and farmland turned to dust. The wheat crop fell to less than half its normal yield. Field trials of wheat genetically modified to survive droughts better were carried out in Australia in 2007.

In Parkes, 186.4 miles (300 km) from Sydney, Australia, land normally underwater is cracked and baked by drought.

crop was a tobacco plant genetically modified to make it resistant to an antibiotic in 1983. The first commercial GM plant, a tomato, was created in 1994. The first GM product to go on sale in shops was a tomato paste made from GM tomatoes in 1996.

Which crops are GM? The most widespread GM crops are soybean, maize (corn), cotton, and oilseed rape (also known as canola). One reason for modifying them is to make them more resistant to pests so that less pest-killing chemicals have to be used on them.

Some crops are modified so that they are resistant to weed-killing chemicals. Chemicals can then be used to wipe out weeds without killing the crop.

By 2006, GM crops were growing on about 252 million acres (102 million ha) of land in 22 countries worldwide, with the area increasing at the rate of about 25 million acres (10 million ha) a year. The biggest GM crop is soybean. More than two-thirds of all the world's soybeans are genetically modified.

Safe to eat? Producers of GM crops say they are safe, because they are thoroughly tested in laboratories and

FOR AND AGAINST

For
- Genetic modification produces drought-resistant and pest-resistant crops.
- Increases crop yields and feeds more people.

Against
- Long-term health effects are unknown.
- May contaminate non-GM crops.
- Could change in unknown ways.

field trials. Critics say that GM crops are not necessary, because traditional breeding methods can produce all the food we need. Critics say the development of GM crops that resist powerful weed killers and pesticides may lead to environmental damage from the chemicals or perhaps the appearance of super-pests and super-weeds. They also say there is a danger of GM crops causing unexpected reactions in people who eat them. One example they give is a variety of GM soy that was given a gene from Brazil nuts in 1995. Scientists testing the soy at the University of Nebraska discovered that people who were allergic to nuts were also allergic to the soy. The gene was removed. In 2005, research in Australia to develop a new pea plant with resistance to a pest called the pea weevil was halted

These soybeans have been genetically modified to resist weed killer, so that weeds can be killed without harming the crop.

WHAT'S NEXT?

In 2006, scientists from the Harvard Medical School, the University of Missouri, and the University of Pittsburgh Medical Center announced that they had inserted a gene from tiny roundworms into pigs. The result was pigs that produced meat containing omega-3 fatty acids, which are good for the heart and circulation of people eating the meat. In the next few years, they will perfect their techniques in pigs and then move on to do the same thing in cows. It means that in the future, people with fatty diets, which result in heart disease today, may be able to eat a healthier diet without having to give up favorite foods such as bacon or steak.

because the new peas caused lung problems in mice. GM producers say this shows that the testing system works.

Changing animals Deciding which farm animals should be allowed to breed together involves guesswork. If breeders had a genetic map of the animals, they could make selective breeding more scientific. They could develop tests to find out which animals have which genes. Then animals with useful genes could be bred together. The complete genetic map of an organism is called its genome. The genomes of the chicken and the cow have already been mapped. Others will follow.

Genetically modified pigs, sheep, and cows have already been created. The first transgenic farm animals (animals with genes from another organism)

The pig with the yellow-green snout is a transgenic pig produced for medical research by adding protein from a jellyfish to its DNA.

were produced for medical research. The first transgenic sheep, Tracy, was produced in Britain in 1991 by PPL Therapeutics. Its human genes produced milk containing human proteins for treating cystic fibrosis and emphysema in humans. The first transgenic pig was also produced in Britain in 1992 by Imutran. Its cells had genetic "flags," or markers, added to them that said "I am human" instead of "I am a pig." Scientists hope this research will lead to transgenic pigs with organs that can be transplanted into humans. Rosie, the first transgenic cow, was produced in 1997. It produced milk with human protein that makes it safer than normal cow's milk for feeding to very young human babies.

Most genetically modified animals are still created for medical research. Dr. Helen Sang at the Roslin Institute in Scotland has inserted human genes into hens so that they lay eggs containing cancer-fighting drugs. These drugs are usually produced by industry at great expense. In the future, hens could be doing the work for the cost of a handful of corn every day.

GM foods on sale There is still a great deal of suspicion and caution among the public about GM foods. Meat and milk from GM animals and fresh GM fruit and vegetables are not on sale in the stores yet, but processed foods such as GM tomato paste are. Farm animals are sometimes given food made from GM crops. As a result of public concern about GM foods, some supermarkets will not sell food products from GM-fed animals.

People demonstrate their opposition to genetically modified organisms in street protests like this one in Montreal, Canada.

A German Greenpeace activist cuts off a sample of genetically modified maize plants in order to analyze them in a lab.

Do genes change by themselves? Scientists don't always have to change an animal's genes. They sometimes stumble upon a lucky accident of nature. Plants and animals usually inherit half of their genes from each parent, so the genetic makeup of plants and animals is mixed in a different way with each new generation. In 2001, scientists in New Zealand found a cow, called Marge, with a gene that made it produce skim milk! Skim milk is healthier, because it contains less fat than normal whole milk. It is usually made by removing fat from whole milk. Butter made from whole milk has to be warmed after it is taken from a fridge before it will spread, but Marge's low-fat butter is spreadable straight from the fridge. Marge's calves were tested and they have the same gene. They produce low-fat milk too. The plan is to breed herds of cows with this same gene. The first low-fat milk and spreadable butter from them could be in the stores by 2011.

Tough tests In 2006, scientists in Australia developed genetic tests that can tell how tough a cow's meat will be to eat and even what the pattern of meat and fat, called marbling, will look like. Good marbling produces succulent cooked meat. A few hairs are plucked from the cow's tail and the DNA for the tests is extracted from the hair roots. In the future, these tests will enable cattle breeders to improve the quality of meat on the dinner table by removing cattle from breeding programs if tests show that they have the genes for tough meat.

This scientist at the U.S. Meat Animal Research Center in Nebraska is examining a farm animal's DNA.

Pharming Because of the public opposition to GM food crops, the next generation of GM farm crops will be grown to produce drugs and vaccines instead of food. This is known as "pharming" (from pharmaceutical farming). In 2006, genetically modified tobacco plants were developed in England to produce a drug that helps prevent HIV. When the crop is harvested, the drug is collected. If the trial is a success, each plant will produce enough of the drug to protect an HIV sufferer for up to three months. It could be a way to supply cheap HIV drugs to African countries. More than half of the world's HIV sufferers live in Africa. Human trials of drugs produced from the plants could begin by 2009. The team is already looking for ways to increase the drug output. One way is to grow the plants in water instead of soil. Instead of harvesting plants and crushing them to expose the drug, the drug simply diffuses into the water.

What is wrong with pharming?
Opponents of pharming worry that plants engineered to produce drugs could escape from greenhouses and alter wild plants, especially food crops. The greenhouses have to be airtight to stop dust-like pollen from the GM plants from being blown outside on air currents.

CHAPTER 2
down on the farm

People have been farming for about 10,000 years. Farms and farming methods changed very little for most of that time. Now, developments in genetics, robotics, and information technology mean that farms and farming methods are changing faster than ever.

SatNav and robots Traditional farming uses knowledge and experience built up over generations of working on the land. Today, farmers also use science and technology to make farms more efficient. Tractors fitted with satellite navigation can steer themselves around fields. They can use the same technology to make maps of the crop yield for each field, and then use this information to adjust the amount of fertilizer given to each part of a field. Some farmers are going even further and using robots.

Farm robots People have been replaced by robots and other machines in many industries. In car factories, for example, robots now do a lot of the work that was once done by people.

This robot is designed to cut grass. A group of robots will swarm over a field to ensure that all the grass is cut as quickly as possible.

The same thing is beginning to happen in farming. Robots are already cutting grass, picking fruit, and milking cows on some farms.

A typical farm robot looks like a small car or buggy with no driver. Grass-cutting robots make a map of a field and then set off to cut the grass all by themselves. Robots for harvesting crops are more complicated. A fruit-picking robot makes a map of each tree and pinpoints the position of every piece of fruit. The robot's arms then use this information to reach out and gently pick the fruit. Vision Robotics in California, is developing these fruit-picking robots. They started developing robots to pick oranges. Now, growers of crops ranging from cherries to asparagus are showing interest in using robots to harvest their crops, too.

Rice robot In 2005, a rice-planting robot was tested in Japan by the National Agricultural Research Center of the National Agriculture and Bio-oriented Research Organization. It worked by laying mats of preplanted rice seedlings in muddy paddy fields. Rice planting is a backbreaking job that few people are prepared to do today, so strong demand is expected for robots that can do the job.

WHAT'S NEXT?

The most difficult crops to pick are very soft crops like mushrooms, because they are so easily damaged. Scientists in Warwick, England, have built a robot that can pick mushrooms. It uses an arm with a suction cup on the end. It works more slowly than a human picker, but a robot can work 24 hours a day.

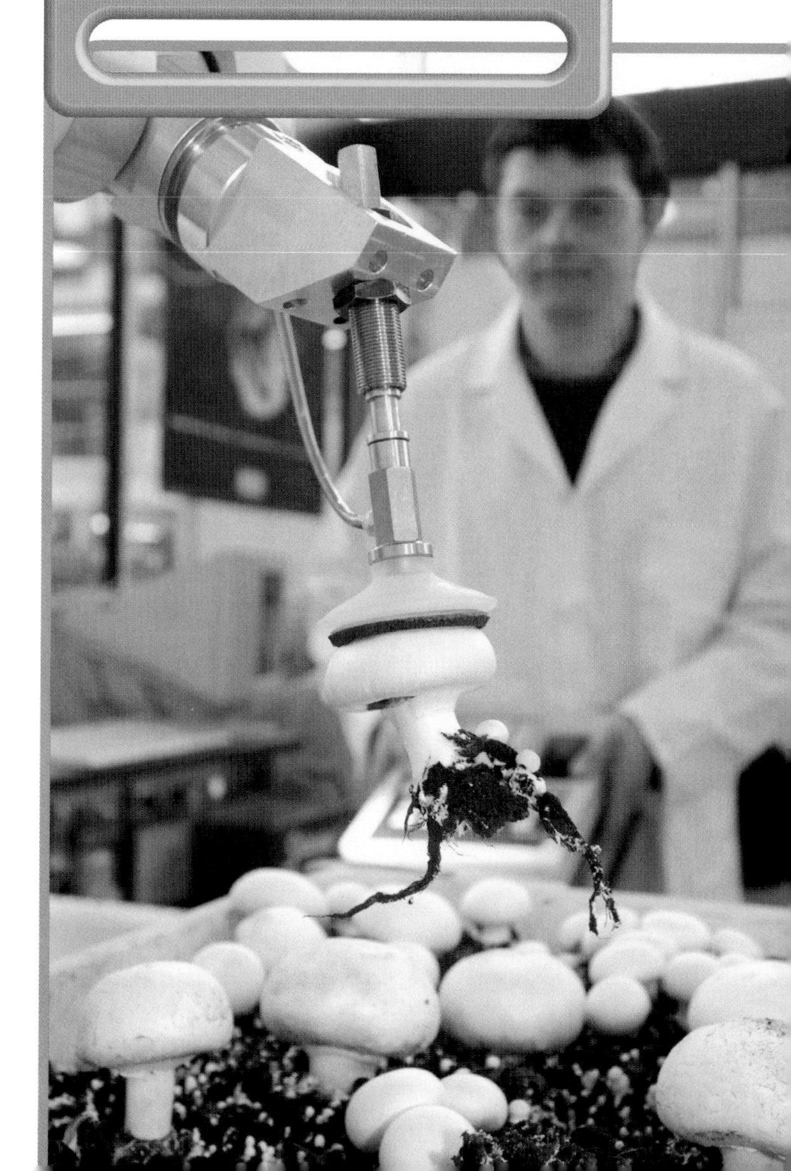

This robot for picking mushrooms was developed at Warwick University, England.

Milking robots Robots are already milking cows on some farms. Robot milking was developed in the Netherlands in the early 1990s. It was used in North America for the first time on a Canadian farm in 1998. Soon afterward, a farm in Wisconsin became the first U.S. farm to try the robots. Mason Dixon Farms in Gettysburg, Pennsylvania, has installed 10 robots to milk 500 of its 2,100 cows. Each robot does about 175 milkings every day. The robots have reduced the farm's labor costs by 75 percent and increased milk production by 15 percent.

Cows at the modern urban farm of Deltapark in Rotterdam, the Netherlands, are milked by robots.

HOW IT WORKS

When a cow comes to a milking station, the robot identifies the cow by reading an electronic tag on its collar. It finds the cow's udder by scanning the cow with a laser. The udder is then cleaned and suction tubes are attached. Suction draws the milk out and pipes it to a storage tank. If the robot has a problem, it can even call the farmer's mobile phone! By the end of 2006, only 1 percent of U.S. dairy farms were using milking robots, mainly because farms invest in major machinery upgrades only every 10-20 years, but the numbers of robots used on farms are expected to increase rapidly.

The agricultural robot developed at the University of Illinois with its creators. "Ag robots" have sensors to detect where a row of crops ends; then they automatically turn. The SICK logo refers to the company that made the laser scanner for this robot, which helps guide it!

Global warming As farm animals digest food, they produce a gas called methane. Methane is a powerful greenhouse gas. When it is released into the air, it traps heat from the Sun and warms the atmosphere. There is great concern about how global warming is changing the Earth's weather. About one-fifth of all the methane produced worldwide comes from farm animals. Nearly all of the methane released in New Zealand comes from the country's 45 million sheep and 10 million cows.

WHAT'S NEXT?

Agricultural engineers at the University of Illinois, Urbana-Champaign, want to replace one big robot moving up and down a field with a team of smaller robots. It won't matter if one robot breaks down, because the others will take over its work. Small robots could reduce the amount of chemicals sprayed on farms. Instead of spraying a whole field, with chemicals drifting elsewhere in the wind, the robots will be able to "spit" a tiny amount of chemical on an individual plant.

Turning down the gas Scientists in Perth, Australia, have made a vaccine that is injected into sheep to reduce the amount of methane they produce. Scientists in Belgium have found that adding fish oil to sheep food has the same effect. In New Zealand, a cow called Myrtle was fitted with a device that measured the amount of gas it "released." Then Myrtle was given different types of food. When Myrtle ate a plant called legume lotus, her methane output fell by nearly one-fifth. A mixture of these and other methods may be used in the future to reduce the greenhouse gases produced by farming.

Farming in the sky Future farms may be put in the middle of cities . . . in skyscrapers! Farming in a skyscraper is also called vertical farming. Vertical farms take up much less space than traditional farms. Professor Dickson Despommier and his students at Columbia University, who came up with the idea of the vertical farm, have determined that a vertical farm producing enough food for 35,000 people would take up only 1/300 of the ground needed for a normal farm. If funding can be found, the first experimental farm could be in operation within about 10 years.

Sheep release methane, a greenhouse gas that contributes to global warming.

A future vertical farm might look like this glass tower.

HOW IT WORKS

The skyscraper has glass walls to let lots of light in. Each floor is an indoor field, where crops grow all year round. Producing fruit, vegetables, and meat in the middle of a city means that the produce wouldn't have to be transported long distances and so there would be no transportation costs or air pollution from the big trucks normally used to transport farm produce.

Farms in the sea Most of the fish that people eat are wild fish caught by boats with nets or lines. The rest comes from fish farms. In the future, more of the world's food needs will be met by fish farming, also known as aquaculture. The United Nations estimates that aquaculture will provide more than half of all the seafood we eat 25 years from now.

A fish farm is a set of floating cages containing fish. Sea water flows through the cages. Fish farms are set up in sheltered water near the seashore—in Norwegian fjords, and sea lochs on the coasts of Scotland and Canada.

Fish farms can reduce the price of fish that used to be very expensive, such as salmon. They can also make up for falling fish catches of popular fish, such as cod and herring. Fish catches are falling because of overfishing and climate change.

Are there any problems with fish farms? Fish farms affect the plants, animals, and water around them. Uneaten fish food and waste from the fish add nutrients to the water, which feed nearby plants and creatures. This alters the natural balance of life in the water. In addition, fish in the cages are so close together that pests and diseases

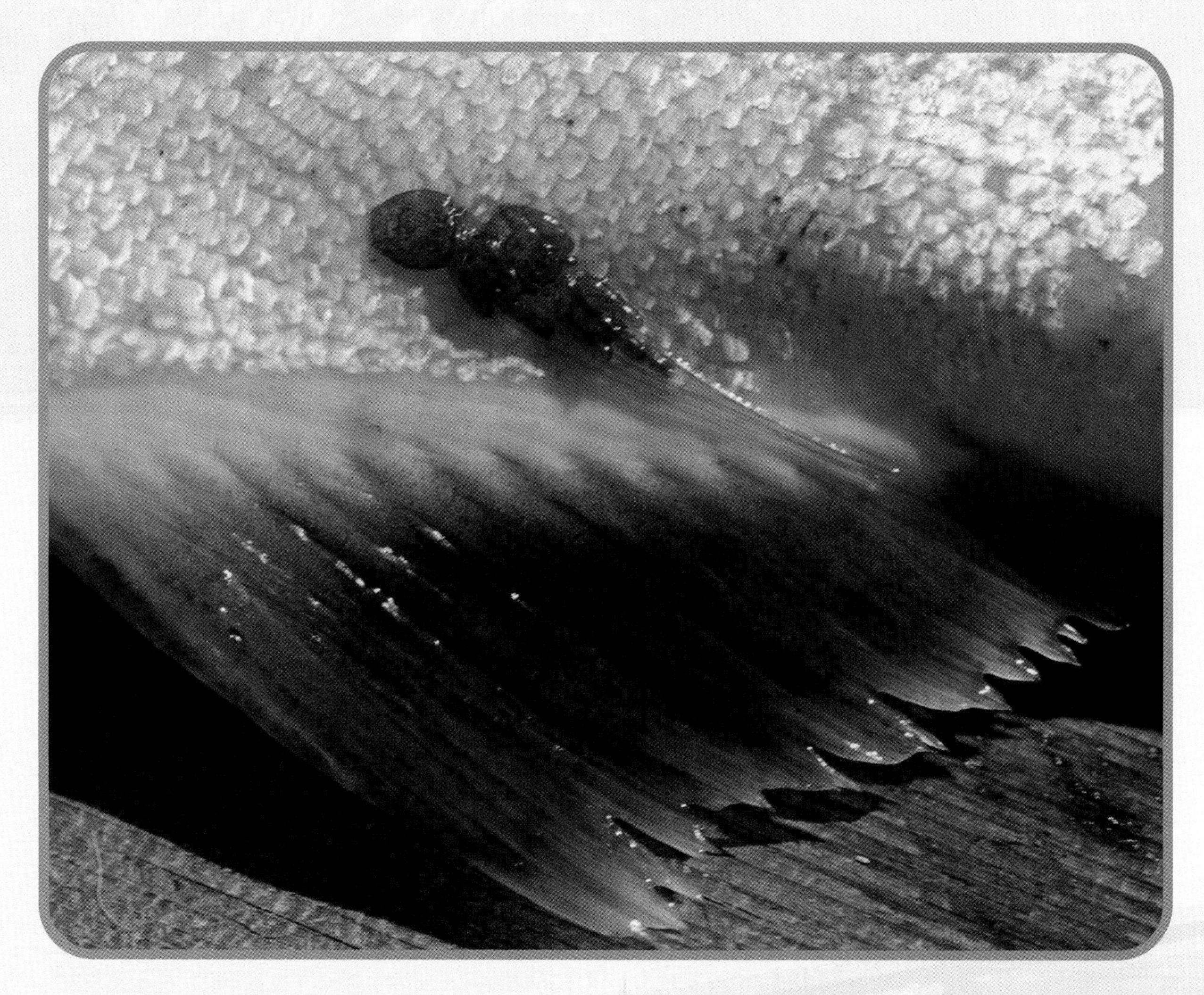

Pests like this sea louse, attached to a salmon, can be a serious problem in fish farms.

spread easily from fish, to fish. They can infect wild fish, too. Pests called sea lice are a problem in salmon. Wild salmon live in the sea, but return to freshwater rivers to spawn. Sea lice cannot live in fresh water, so they are not a serious problem in wild salmon. However, farmed salmon spend their whole life in seawater, which allows the lice to spread and multiply. They can also spread to wild salmon passing by. In one year, nearly all the wild salmon in one Norwegian fjord died because of sea lice. Wild salmon off the Canadian coast have been badly affected, too.

Environmentally friendly fish farming Scientists are developing new ways of farming fish that do not harm the environment. Scientists at the University of Miami have experimented with sinking fish cages far deeper than

This fish farm floats in the calm, sheltered waters of a Norwegian fjord.

usual—as deep as 98 feet (30 m). Here, stronger currents flow through the cages and flush away uneaten food and waste that would normally collect underneath them. Researchers at the University of New Brunswick, Canada, are experimenting with "self-cleaning" fish farms by mixing different species in the same farm. One species feeds on the waste of the next species. They found that mussels (shellfish) and kelp (seaweed) thrived near salmon cages and cleaned up their waste.

WHAT'S NEXT?

Future fish farms could be floating free at sea. In the open sea, the cages could be bigger and farther apart. With more space between the fish, pests and diseases would not spread as easily. These fish farms would be able to move. They could sink deeper in the water if a storm or a ship came toward them. This sounds like science fiction, but work is already underway in Norway.

CHAPTER 3
functional foods

Most processed foods today are enriched or fortified with extra vitamins or minerals to make them more nutritious. Functional foods go one step further. They contain substances that help improve health or prevent illness.

Nutraceuticals People have made claims about the health effects of foods for about 150 years. These early claims were unreliable because they were anecdotal—they relied on how well people said they felt after eating certain foods. Now, the health effects of foods and their ingredients can be tested scientifically. Some foods do have a good effect on people's health. Some of them can even help to prevent serious illnesses. The substances added to foods to improve health are sometimes called "nutraceuticals." The foods are also known as functional foods, designer foods, clever foods, or techno-foods. Sales of these foods are growing rapidly. Many people like the idea of improving their health and preventing diseases by eating special foods instead of taking medicines. The term "nutraceutical" was invented in 1989 by Dr. Stephen DeFelice. The word

Bread is commonly fortified with calcium, an important mineral for the formation and continuing strength of our bones.

This scientist is adding folate (folic acid or vitamin B9) to a dish of applesauce. Folic acid is an important food supplement.

"nutraceutical" is used to describe a food ingredient or a food that is claimed to have a medicine-like effect.

Early days Work on boosting the nutritional and health value of food began seriously in the 1930s. For good health, the human body needs the right amounts of protein, carbohydrates, and fat, plus water and small amounts of vitamins and minerals. Even in wealthy, developed countries in the 1930s, people had such a poor diet that serious illnesses and even deaths caused by vitamin and mineral deficiencies were common. So, vitamins and minerals were added to foods such as bread and breakfast cereals. Since then, many more foods have been fortified with extra vitamins or minerals. Vitamin D may be added to milk to prevent a disease called rickets that causes deformities in bones. Vitamin C and calcium are added to fruit juices. Vitamins B1 and B3, iron, and calcium are added to flour.

Super-tomatoes Ordinary foods can be modified genetically or specially bred to transform them into foods with a good effect on health. Tomatoes are known to help prevent some cancers.

HELPING BABIES

A vitamin called folic acid is added to flour and bread in some countries, including the U.S., Canada, and Chile. It is added to help prevent problems called neural-tube defects, which affect the development of a baby's brain and spinal cord. The effects of folic acid have been known for a long time, but surveys show that many women are still unaware of how important it is. Adding it to flour and bread ensures that everyone receives some.

Tomatoes contain an anticancer substance called lycopene, which can be boosted to higher levels by selective breeding or genetic engineering.

One study found that men eating 10 or more servings of tomatoes or tomato sauce every week lowered their risk of developing prostate cancer by 45 percent. The substance in tomatoes that protects from cancer is called lycopene. It gives tomatoes their red color. It is thought to protect cells in the body from damage. Cancer is caused by cells going wrong and multiplying out of control, producing a tumor. Protecting cells from damage may help stop this uncontrolled growth from starting.

Now, a super-tomato has been developed with twice the normal amount of lycopene. It was developed in the Netherlands by selective breeding from different types of tomatoes with high levels of lycopene. It went on sale in Britain in 2006. Another high-lycopene tomato has been developed by researchers at Purdue University, Indiana, and the U.S. Department of Agriculture (USDA). They used genetic engineering to boost the lycopene to more than three the times normal level. This tomato will probably not be in the stores for several years.

Brain food? One of the most popular dietary supplements today is omega-3. Research has found that omega-3 fatty acids reduce the risk of heart disease, lower blood pressure, and help stop blood vessels from clogging up inside.

These capsules contain fish oil, a source of omega-3 fatty acids.

They also seem to help electrical signals travel from cell to cell in the brain. The body cannot make omega-3 fatty acids. They have to come from our diet. They are found in foods including oily fish such as mackerel, salmon, tuna, and sardines. People are eating less oily fish today, so to make up for this, some

WHAT'S NEXT?

Today, functional foods deliver substances in food to the whole body. In the future, perhaps using genetic engineering, it may be possible to target certain nutraceuticals at particular organs or tissues in the body, so that only those organs or tissues are affected.

margarines, yogurts, and eggs are enriched with extra omega-3.

Cutting cholesterol In the 1990s, research in Finland showed that substances called phytosterols, found in plants, could reduce a fat called cholesterol found in the blood. Cholesterol is essential for good health, but too much of the wrong sort of cholesterol can cause heart disease and clog arteries. Most cholesterol is made in the body, but some comes from food.

This scan shows an artery which has become dangerously narrowed by a thick, fatty lining, caused by high levels of cholesterol in the blood.

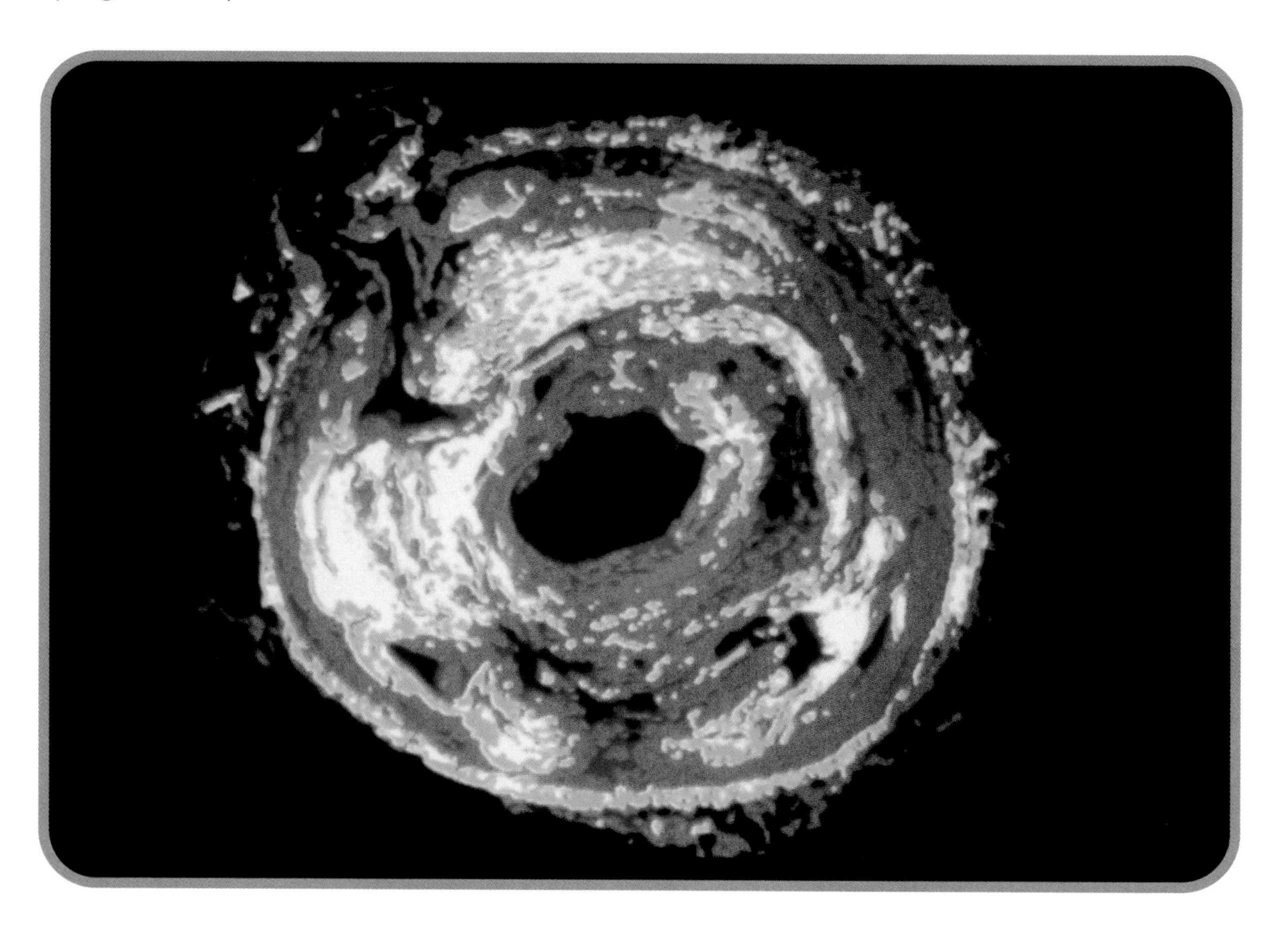

HOW IT WORKS

Nutraceuticals such as phytosterols are extracted from plants by dissolving them out. A solvent is mixed with mashed-up plants to dissolve the substance and wash it out of the plant. Different solvents dissolve different substances. Another method uses carbon dioxide gas. At about 800 times the normal atmospheric pressure, carbon dioxide behaves like a liquid. The precise pressure and temperature are chosen to suit the substance to be extracted. When it is injected into a plant, it separates out the substance. This method is called supercritical fluid extraction.

PRE & PROBIOTICS

Prebiotics and probiotics are increasingly popular functional foods. They aim to improve digestion by acting on the bacteria in the gut. Food is digested by digestive juices produced by the body and bacteria in the gut. There are all sorts of bacteria. Some are good for digesting food. Others are not. The types and amounts of bacteria in the gut can be upset by illness, stress, and some medicines. Prebiotics and probiotics claim to build up the numbers of good bacteria. Prebiotics are starchy substances that are not digested themselves, but they encourage the growth of good bacteria. Probiotics contain live bacteria that travel to the gut, where they help to digest food. Probiotics are often eaten in the form of yogurt.

The fatty diets that many people have today supply too much of the wrong type of cholesterol. Phytosterols reduce the amount of cholesterol absorbed from food by the blood, and so reduce the health problems it causes. Some margarines and yogurts are now enriched with phytosterols.

Good or bad? Functional foods are not medicines, so they do not have to be tested like medicines. As a result, the scientific evidence for some of the claims made for functional foods may be very weak. Adding substances to foods to improve health or prevent illness is supported by many people, but many others are opposed to it. They say it amounts to mass medication. There are strict regulations covering the manufacturing and use of medicines, but governments have been very slow to issue regulations to control nutraceuticals and functional foods.

CHAPTER 4
nanotech

Nanotechnology is the technology of making and using particles so small that they can only be seen by using a powerful microscope. Nanotechnology is becoming increasingly important—and controversial—in food technology.

Nanotechnology is already used to make hundreds of nonfood products, including cosmetics and paints. Now, hundreds of companies all over the world are busy developing nano-products for the food industry.

"Nano" means one-billionth. The size of nanoparticles is measured in nanometers, or billionths of a meter.

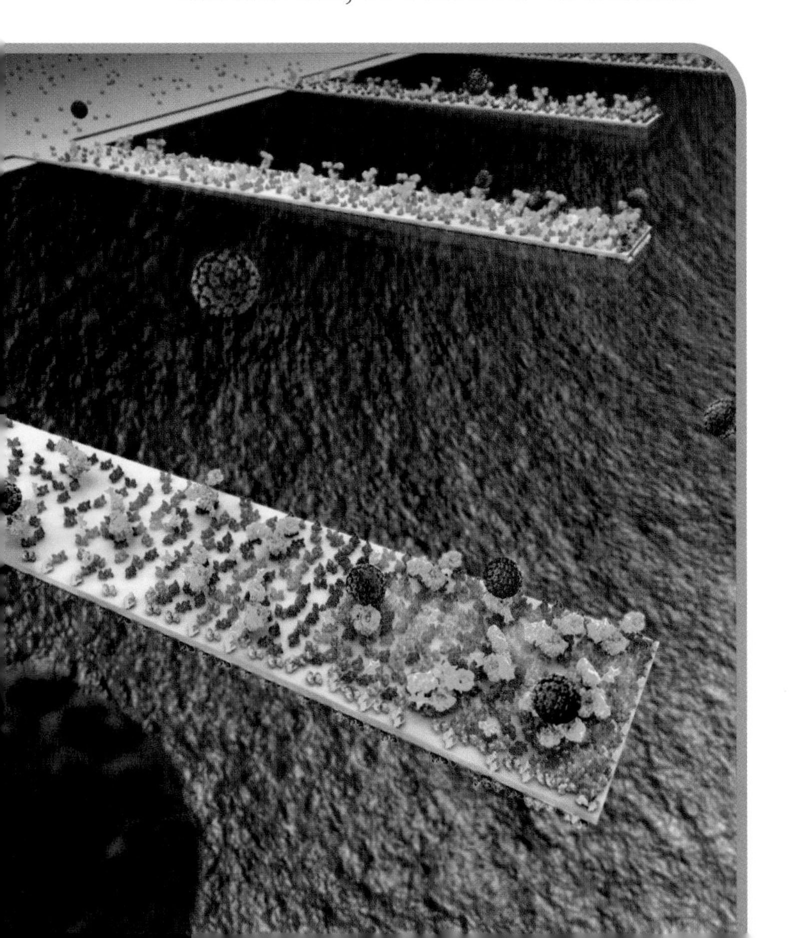

Nanotechnology makes use of particles up to about 100 nanometers across. You could fit 1,000 particles this size across the width of a human hair!

Nanotechnology is being developed in the food industry because it can make food safer by reducing the risks from harmful bacteria. It can also reduce the amount of fat that various foods contain without changing their flavor.

Nanofilters Liquids are often purified by running them through a filter so that solid particles are trapped by the filter. Nanofilters, filters made from nanoparticles, are so incredibly fine that they even trap bacteria. Nanofilters are already being used to remove bacteria from milk. Nanoparticles are also being developed to detect harmful bacteria in meat after it has been packaged. The particles are coated with molecules that

These tiny structures, like diving boards, are nanocantilevers. They could be used to detect dangerous substances, because they vibrate at different speeds when contaminants stick to them.

lock onto certain bacteria. When they link up with the right bacteria, they glow! So, the more harmful bacteria the nanoparticles find and stick to, the brighter the glow.

Keeping clean Cleanliness is essential in places where food is processed. The surfaces food touches must be kept free of bacteria. This is done by washing them with bacteria-killing disinfectants. Using nanotechnology, it is possible to make surfaces that clean themselves. Nature discovered how to do this millions of years ago. The lotus plant has self-cleaning leaves. The waxy leaves are covered with microscopic bumps and hair-like structures. Water droplets roll off the leaves, collecting dirt and bacteria as they go. The secret of the lotus leaf was revealed in 2006 by researchers at the General Motors Research and Development Center in Michigan. Now nanotechnologists are developing self-cleaning surfaces for food processing, by copying the lotus leaf.

A drop of water sits on a water-repellent surface without being absorbed.

HOW IT WORKS

Scientists at the University of Twente in the Netherlands have made a copy of the lotus leaf by using lasers to bombard a surface with microscopic "light bullets." They carve a ripple pattern into the surface and make it water-resistant like a lotus leaf. The German chemical company, BASF, has developed a spray-on coating for surfaces that mimics the lotus leaf and makes them water-resistant or dirt resistant. They are using the same coating to develop a water-repellent cardboard for food packaging, expected to be available by 2009.

Cabbage that tastes like chocolate? Hollow nanoparticles can be filled with substances. This is called "nanoencapsulation." A food can have nanocapsules added, containing a substance that gives the food a different flavor. Keeping the flavoring inside nanocapsules stops it from discoloring the food or reacting with it. Foods that children dislike could be given a more appetizing flavor—cabbage that tastes of chocolate, for example!

Programmable food In 2000, NanoteK, a group of scientists from universities and research laboratories in several countries, embarked on a series of projects, including "programmable food." You decide its color and flavor after you buy it!

In the future, programmable drinks will turn whatever flavor you choose. Researchers are also working on drinks that get thicker the more you shake them.

HOW IT WORKS

When you buy a programmable drink, it's clear and tasteless. At home, you put it in a new type of microwave unit or ultrasound unit. The drink contains nanocapsules full of different colors and flavors. Choose one microwave or ultrasound frequency and only the nanocapsules for red color and strawberry flavor burst. Choose another frequency to get an orange drink, or coffee, or cola.

Reducing fat Reducing the amount of fat in food makes it healthier, but it also changes the flavor of the food and the way it feels in your mouth. Scientists in the Netherlands are using nanotechnology to reduce the amount of fat in food without changing its flavor or texture. They are making a new type of mayonnaise. Mayonnaise is usually a very fatty sauce. The fat is in the form of tiny droplets of oil. The Dutch scientists have created nanodroplets that are oil on the outside, but water inside.

Dangers? Nanotechnology can produce tastier, healthier food, but there may be risks, too. Nanoparticles are so small that they can get inside living cells. Once inside a cell, they can even move into the cell's nucleus, where its DNA is located. Scientists have already seen human cells with nanoparticles inside the nucleus. The effects of nanoparticles on DNA are unknown. Worries about possible health risks may keep some people from eating nanofoods, just as they have kept them from eating GM foods.

FOR AND AGAINST

For

- Nanotechnology can boost flavor, color, and nutrition.
- Can keep food fresher for longer.
- Can improve hygiene in factories.

Against

- Takes food further away from nature.
- Health effects unknown.
- Genetic effects unknown.

Mayonnaise made with nanodroplets of oil contains less fat than normal.

CHAPTER 5
packaging and preserving

Today food packaging is increasingly high tech and clever. It can protect food from contamination and keep food from spoiling for many years. It can even heat food up or cool food down when the package is opened. New labels can keep track of food with radio signals.

In the past, food was grown, harvested, processed, and sold very quickly, because it didn't travel very far. It was often sold unwrapped. Today, food starts its journey to the table from all over the world. Good packaging is essential to protect it from damage and contamination and keep it in good condition. Figures from the World Health Organization show that food wastage in the developing world can be as high as 50 percent, while good packaging reduces wastage in developed countries to 3 percent or less.

Packaging is essential in the food industry today, to keep food clean and undamaged.

Improving packaging Packets, cans, and bottles contain much less material than they used to in the past. A drink can in the 1950s was more than four times heavier than the same can today. In the same time, a glass milk bottle has shed half of its weight. Plastic bottles are lighter, too. Using less material to make each package and encouraging people to recycle as much packaging as possible saves energy and materials, and reduces the amount of waste that has to be disposed of.

Edible packaging One way to reduce the amount of food packaging waste is to eat the packaging! Dr. Tara McHugh at the USDA has developed edible packaging. It could help to reduce the mountain of 169.5 million tons (153.8 million t) of waste that currently go to U.S. landfills every year. Even if the wrappers aren't eaten, they are completely biodegradable.

HOW IT WORKS

The USDA edible packaging is made from a soup of mashed fruit or vegetables formed into sheets and dried to make a thin plastic-like film only .004 inches (.10 mm) thick. Cellulose and pectin, natural substances in fruit and vegetables, give the film its strength. So far, edible packaging has been made from apples, strawberries, peaches, carrots, and broccoli.

Active packaging Packaging that just wraps food is known as "passive packaging." Packaging that uses special gases or chemistry to keep food fresher for longer is called "active packaging."

Clever design and improved materials mean that plastic bottles contain a lot less plastic now than in the past.